# A WHOLE LIFE

## STUDY GUIDE

Cover design by: Sara Young
Cover photo by: Andrew van Tilborgh

ISBN: 978-1-960678-79-9          1 2 3 4 5 6 7 8 9 10

Printed in the United States of America

JACK JAMESON

# A WHOLE LIFE

*MY PATH FROM HARD-TIME KID TO
HIGH-IMPACT CONSULTANT*

## STUDY GUIDE

FO
UR

# CONTENTS

JACK JAMESON

# A WHOLE LIFE

## MY PATH FROM HARD-TIME KID TO HIGH-IMPACT CONSULTANT

# CHAPTER 1

*If I've learned one thing in life,*
*it's that speculation gets you nowhere.*

## READING TIME

As you read
Chapter 1 in
*A Whole Life*,
reflect on,
and respond
to the text by
answering
the following
questions.

# REFLECT AND TAKE ACTION:

Reflect on the author's experience with his father. Have you ever gotten caught up in ruminating over "whys" and "what ifs"? How did it distract you from moving forward?

_____

_____

_____

_____

_____

_____

_____

_____

_____

_____

What kind of traumatic experiences have shaped your worldview? Have they evolved over time, and in what ways?

_____

_____

_____

_____

_____

_____

_____

_____

_____

_____

Have you ever felt neglected or abandoned by someone you depended on? Explain how this impacted your ability to trust. How well are you able to trust others now?

_____

_____

_____

_____

_____

_____

_____

_____

What role did this experience play in the expectations you set for yourself and other relationships presently? Are those expectations harming or helping you?

_____

_____

_____

_____

_____

_____

_____

_____

_____

What kind of coping mechanisms, both negative and positive, have you or do you employ in response to severe disappointment or betrayal?

_____

_____

_____

_____

_____

_____

_____

_____

_____

Which coping mechanisms do you need to ditch? If you could start with just one, which would it be? What steps can you take today to replace it with healthier, more productive ones?

_____

_____

_____

_____

_____

_____

_____

_____

_____

What kind of "ripple effects" has adversity had on other areas of your life?

_____

_____

_____

_____

_____

_____

_____

_____

Consider the hurts and wounds that have vicariously affected you through the abuse or misuse of someone you love. How do you make sense of that pain now?

_____

_____

_____

_____

_____

_____

_____

_____

_____

# NOTES

_____

_____

_____

_____

_____

_____

_____

_____

_____

_____

_____

_____

_____

_____

_____

_____

_____

_____

_____

_____

_____

_____

_____

_____

_____

_____

# CHAPTER 2

*How does it feel to learn of close blood relatives you never knew about and will never have the chance to meet—at least, this side of heaven? Strangely, not much.*

READING
TIME

As you read
Chapter 2 in
*A Whole Life*,
reflect on,
and respond
to the text by
answering
the following
questions.

# REFLECT AND TAKE ACTION:

What can we learn from the author's story about Garry? How does our finite knowledge of someone else's story contribute to judgment, accusation, and mistreatment?

_____

_____

_____

_____

_____

_____

_____

_____

_____

Gleaning from Garry's background, how do you reconcile the message of rising above adversity for someone who has been dealt an unfair hand?

_____

_____

_____

_____

_____

_____

_____

_____

Putting yourself in the author's shoes, how might learning later in life that your childhood friend was actually your brother have affected you?

_____

_____

_____

_____

_____

_____

_____

_____

The author claims that his mother was the only constant presence in his life. In what ways could a revolving door of relationships shape your only constant relationship?

_____

_____

_____

_____

_____

_____

_____

_____

What do your memories of past experiences with upheaval, chaos, confusion, or instability feel like to you now? How do you experience them?

_____

_____

_____

_____

_____

_____

_____

_____


The author relays his mother's declaration after Garry's death, "Sometimes you kill people with words." What does this mean to you and how has this truth surfaced in your own life?

_____

_____

_____

_____

_____

_____

_____

_____

Have you ever become desensitized to pain and adversity? What do you attribute that to? Elaborate.

_____

_____

_____

_____

_____

_____

_____

_____

Think of someone you know who has made devastating life decisions. What does good decision-making look like when it appears the odds of rising above your circumstances are against you?

_____

_____

_____

_____

_____

_____

_____

_____

# NOTES

_____

_____

_____

_____

_____

_____

_____

_____

_____

_____

_____

_____

_____

_____

_____

_____

_____

_____

_____

_____

_____

_____

_____

# CHAPTER 3

*We often wouldn't eat at all the last few days of the month because we had no money: we were into intermittent fasting before it became a thing, by necessity, not design.*

## READING TIME

As you read Chapter 3 in *A Whole Life*, reflect on, and respond to the text by answering the following questions.

# REFLECT AND TAKE ACTION:

During times of misfortune, what story were you told about your life, identity, and circumstances? How did they impact you?

_____

_____

_____

_____

_____

_____

_____

_____

The author describes his mother's lifestyle with men and the measures he had to take to protect both himself and his sister. Can you relate to this story in any way? How so?

_____

_____

_____

_____

_____

_____

_____

_____

_____

Think of a time when you had to live on little. What practices did you put in place to survive or endure? How has that experience formed who you are today?

_____

_____

_____

_____

_____

_____

_____

_____

_____

Providing a personal example, describe how lack can generate insecurity or shame. How has your perspective of lack changed over the course of your lifetime?

_____

_____

_____

_____

_____

_____

_____

_____

_____

What can you learn from shame? How can you use it to create a life of abundance and joy?

_____

_____

_____

_____

_____

_____

_____

_____

How can confusion and turmoil encourage the justification of negative behaviors?

_____

_____

_____

_____

_____

_____

_____

_____

Consider the author's story about breaking into abandoned properties. Why do you think he chose to rationalize this behavior? What would have happened if he had not?

_____

_____

_____

_____

_____

_____

_____

_____

Why does it become problematic later in life to expect abandonment and continual impermanence?

_____

_____

_____

_____

_____

_____

_____

_____

_____

# NOTES

_____

_____

_____

_____

_____

_____

_____

_____

_____

_____

_____

_____

_____

_____

_____

_____

_____

_____

_____

_____

_____

_____

_____

_____

_____

_____

_____

_____

# CHAPTER 4

*When the kids at school wanted to know what had happened to my new shoes the next week, I told a story about them having been stolen.*

## READING TIME

As you read Chapter 4 in *A Whole Life*, reflect on, and respond to the text by answering the following questions.

# REFLECT AND TAKE ACTION:

The author insinuates that his relationship with his mother was unpredictable. How do relationships characterized by unpredictability extend to future relationships?

_____

_____

_____

_____

_____

_____

_____

_____

What do you make out of the phone interaction about the peeping tom between the author and his mother?

_____

_____

_____

_____

_____

_____

_____

_____

_____

In what ways do you think his mother's girls' trip may have muddied, changed, or reinforced his perspective on how his mother felt about him and his sister?

_____

_____

_____

_____

_____

_____

_____

_____

Think of a TV show or movie that once shaped (or currently shapes) your view about relationships. How do the relationship dynamics compare or contrast to your own relationship(s)?

_____

_____

_____

_____

_____

_____

_____

_____

What kind of emotions or thoughts came up for you as you compared your relationship(s) against those in the TV show or movie you chose?

_____

_____

_____

_____

_____

_____

_____

_____

Have you ever taken hypothetical or fictional relationships and, in your imagination, made them your own? Why or why not?

_____

_____

_____

_____

_____

_____

_____

_____

_____

What other things have you used in an attempt to fill the voids that broken relationships have hollowed? What was the outcome?

_____

_____

_____

_____

_____

_____

_____

_____

_____

How can the encouragement and kindness of just one person, like Aunt Alice, make such a difference for someone who has only known instability? Who is that person for you?

_____

_____

_____

_____

_____

_____

_____

_____

# NOTES

_____

_____

_____

_____

_____

_____

_____

_____

_____

_____

_____

_____

_____

_____

_____

_____

_____

_____

_____

_____

_____

_____

_____

_____

_____

# CHAPTER 5

*I loved the quiet sense of order
that permeated their home.*

# READING TIME

As you read
Chapter 5 in
*A Whole Life*,
reflect on,
and respond
to the text by
answering
the following
questions.

# REFLECT AND TAKE ACTION:

The author speculates whether his home environment was the culprit of his speech problem as a child. What does this say about invisible causes underlying visible problems?

_____

_____

_____

_____

_____

_____

_____

How can you use this discovery to reinterpret your own life or how you view someone else's?

_____

_____

_____

_____

_____

_____

_____

_____

_____

_____

What does the author's story about the joy he felt gifting Miss Berry a locket teach you about the transforming power of giving? What role does it play in elevating our own lives?

_____

_____

_____

_____

_____

_____

_____

How do you think a "yes" (joining Cub Scouts) amid a lifelong trail of "nos" due to limited resources shaped the author's definition of what it means to live a whole life?

_____

_____

_____

_____

_____

_____

_____

How do the small blessings in life (like the author's friend James) help counterbalance the misfortunes? Provide a personal example.

_____

_____

_____

_____

_____

_____

_____

_____

James and his family exposed the author to a functional, orderly home—far different from his own. Who has modeled for you a way of life that has somehow influenced the way you live your life today?

_____

_____

_____

_____

_____

_____

_____

_____

# CHAPTER 6

*The only times I got involved
in wrongdoing as a kid was
when I had no choice.*

**READING TIME**

As you read Chapter 6 in *A Whole Life*, reflect on, and respond to the text by answering the following questions.

# REFLECT AND TAKE ACTION:

In this chapter, Uncle Sonny prepares the author for his "inevitable visit" to prison. What can you learn from this interaction about normalizing and expecting unhealthy familial patterns to persist over generations?

_____

_____

_____

_____

_____

_____

_____

_____

The author's mother denied Uncle Sonny was the one pictured on the FBI's Ten Most Wanted list. Why do you think she denied it? What purpose did it serve, if any?

_____

_____

_____

_____

_____

_____

_____

_____

Have you ever caught yourself assuming that someone is destined to take the "crooked path" because of the transgressions or dysfunction of other family members? Provide an example.

_____

_____

_____

_____

_____

_____

_____

_____

_____

_____

Why do you think some children who grow up in a stressful environment take a better path later in life and others repeat the dysfunctional patterns of their families?

_____

_____

_____

_____

_____

_____

_____

_____

_____

_____

What kind of relationship dynamics do you find odd or unhealthy in your own family? In what ways do you fixate on them? In what ways have you learned to let them go?

_____

_____

_____

_____

_____

_____

_____

_____

_____

_____

_____

_____

# CHAPTER 7

*Some kids suffer unspeakable abuse;*
*adults use them in ways that can*
*scar their hearts and sear their souls*
*such that only a miracle can heal.*

As you read
Chapter 7 in
*A Whole Life*,
reflect on,
and respond
to the text by
answering
the following
questions.

# REFLECT AND TAKE ACTION:

Think of a time in your life when God's hand of protection was most evident. How has this revelation shaped your relationship with God? What did you learn about Him that you didn't know before?

_____

_____

_____

_____

_____

_____

_____

_____

_____

Where do you think God was in the lives of others who did not fare as well as the author?

_____

_____

_____

_____

_____

_____

_____

_____

_____

Where do we find hope in God's mercy and protection in a world with no guarantees?

_____

_____

_____

_____

_____

_____

_____

_____

How did God use the author's early exposure to violence, abuse, and infidelity for his good?

_____

_____

_____

_____

_____

_____

_____

_____

What kind of image of men do you think the author was forming throughout the course of his life? How have your own encounters with people colored your worldview and what does it take to create new ones?

_____

_____

_____

_____

_____

_____

_____

The author tells of his miraculous ability to reject temptation and escape irreversible damage despite the odds stacked against him. How did the author's internal characteristics and external support systems play a role in his resilience?

_____

_____

_____

_____

_____

_____

_____

_____

# CHAPTER 8

These sorts of splashes of goodness
didn't just come from unexpected places;
they also came from unlikely people.

READING
TIME

As you read
Chapter 8 in
*A Whole Life*
reflect on,
and respond
to the text by
answering
the following
questions.

# REFLECT AND TAKE ACTION:

Consider the Fireside Rec center that became the author's refuge from chaos. Where do you find refuge? In what ways does it offer unique solace?

_____

_____

_____

_____

_____

_____

_____

Describe when and how God has used unlikely people in unlikely places to accomplish something bigger than you. Reflecting on what you can remember, what do you think God accomplished through those relationships?

_____

_____

_____

_____

_____

_____

_____

_____

_____

Reflect on the author's relationship with Frank and Fred. Do you have a Frank or Fred in your life? In what ways has that person changed you?

_____

_____

_____

_____

_____

_____

_____

_____

_____

Have you ever been a Frank or Fred to someone else? In what ways did you impact their lives?

_____

_____

_____

_____

_____

_____

_____

_____

_____

_____

How does the collection of stories in this chapter illustrate the existence and sovereignty of God over our circumstances?

_____

_____

_____

_____

_____

_____

_____

_____

_____

_____

_____

_____

# CHAPTER 9

One lesson I learned both from
watching the way Mom lived and
from my own experiences was not to
try to hold on to things too tightly.

As you read
Chapter 9 in
*A Whole Life*,
reflect on,
and respond
to the text by
answering
the following
questions.

# REFLECT AND TAKE ACTION:

Bring to mind someone who has hurt you deeply in the past. What are three good things that came out of that experience? Can you find any good qualities in that person? What are they?

_____

_____

_____

_____

_____

_____

_____

_____

What do you think the author means when he says to try not to "hold on to things too tightly" in light of the burdens we carry and the obstacles we face? Provide a personal example.

_____

_____

_____

_____

_____

_____

_____

_____

_____

Is there anything you're holding onto too tightly? Ask God what you need to give over to Him.

_____

_____

_____

_____

_____

_____

_____

_____

_____

_____

Consider the author's story about the fire his sister, Tracy, accidentally started. Did you learn anything new about his mother? If so, what, and how can you apply it to your own relationships?

_____

_____

_____

_____

_____

_____

_____

_____

_____

_____

_____

What kind of coping strategies (both positive and negative) have you used throughout your lifetime to forget about or quieten disorder and pain? How have those strategies evolved over time?

_____

_____

_____

_____

_____

_____

_____

_____

_____

_____

_____

# CHAPTER 10

*And, sure enough, as I kept exploring,
I discovered something that made me
feel really alive—at least fleetingly.*

## READING TIME

As you read
Chapter 10 in
*A Whole Life*,
reflect on,
and respond
to the text by
answering
the following
questions.

# REFLECT AND TAKE ACTION:

Have you ever had an important authority figure encourage or engage in self-destructive behaviors with you? What did you learn from it?

_____

_____

_____

_____

_____

_____

_____

_____

_____

Compare and contrast the impact that participating in harmful behaviors with peers to participating with a caregiver or other important authority figure has had on you or someone you know.

_____

_____

_____

_____

_____

_____

_____

_____

What role have your social influences, both past and present, played in your decision-making now?

_____

_____

_____

_____

_____

_____

_____

_____

_____

_____

In what ways has your story impacted others, both negatively and positively? What pieces of your story need to come with you, and what pieces need to be left behind?

_____

_____

_____

_____

_____

_____

_____

_____

_____

_____

_____

Think of a time when you ignored the counsel of the "small voice" inside of you. What were the consequences? Why did you ignore it?

_____

_____

_____

_____

_____

_____

_____

_____

_____

_____

_____

# CHAPTER 11

*I sailed through the rest of the night, loving how it felt to hold people's attention and channel their mood.*

## READING TIME

As you read
Chapter 11 in
*A Whole Life*,
reflect on,
and respond
to the text by
answering
the following
questions.

# REFLECT AND TAKE ACTION:

Consider the author's response to his new bike being stolen. How did it differ from his response to past losses? What do you think accounts for this difference?

_____

_____

_____

_____

_____

_____

_____

_____

_____

Reflect on the ways the author's adopted father, Royce, treated the author and his siblings. How do you think a child would interpret this behavior?

_____

_____

_____

_____

_____

_____

_____

_____

_____

Where do you see God's hand in the family's move to
Louisiana?

_____

_____

_____

_____

_____

_____

_____

_____

_____

_____

Have you ever felt God's presence and grace in the midst
of chaos? Describe that experience in detail. What kind of
myths about hardship did that experience expose?

_____

_____

_____

_____

_____

_____

_____

_____

_____

_____

Recall a time when you felt noticed and appreciated. In what ways, if any, did this experience initiate a healing process for you? What needed healing?

_____

_____

_____

_____

_____

_____

_____

_____

_____

_____

_____

# CHAPTER 12

Someone was looking out for
me, like those nights when I
had been gently prevented from
wandering out of my bedroom.

## READING TIME

As you read Chapter 12 in *A Whole Life*, reflect on, and respond to the text by answering the following questions.

# REFLECT AND TAKE ACTION:

Where do you think the author's mother's beliefs about Christianity and Christians came from? Can you relate, and in what ways?

_____

_____

_____

_____

_____

_____

_____

_____

_____

What does the author's introduction to Christianity say about God's ability to work outside of our awareness? What kind of observations have you made about God's "quiet" hand in your life?

_____

_____

_____

_____

_____

_____

_____

_____

_____

_____

Consider the author's dream of Babe and his encounter with the voice of God. What do you think God was thanking him for?

_____

_____

_____

_____

_____

_____

_____

_____

_____

Reflect on the author's dream about his encounter with Jesus in the cafeteria. What stood out to you, and why?

_____

_____

_____

_____

_____

_____

_____

_____

Can you remember when you began to recognize blessings in your own life as God's protection and favor? What did that discovery look like? Was it gradual? Sudden?

_____

_____

_____

_____

_____

_____

_____

What did Scott and his mother's response teach you about God—His heart and His character? How did they exemplify those qualities on the day of the car wreck?

_____

_____

_____

_____

_____

_____

_____

_____

# CHAPTER 13

*I may not have achieved much by other people's standards up to this point, but I had prided myself on at least being able to take care of myself. I'd never been a quitter.*

## READING TIME

As you read Chapter 13 in *A Whole Life*, reflect on, and respond to the text by answering the following questions.

# REFLECT AND TAKE ACTION:

How has adversity aided in the discovery of your gifts?

_____

_____

_____

_____

_____

_____

_____

_____

_____

Have you ever used a good thing (e.g., the author's new job or the nice house he got to live in) to fund or fuel a bad habit? Explain.

_____

_____

_____

_____

_____

_____

_____

_____

_____

_____

Describe the pivotal moment when you grew sick of a self-destructive habit or pattern. What did you do and what was the outcome?

_____

_____

_____

_____

_____

_____

_____

_____

_____

In what way does self-sabotage play a role in your decision making? Would your life look different if you didn't allow self-sabotage to be part of your decisions?

_____

_____

_____

_____

_____

_____

_____

_____

Think of a time when you squandered an opportunity through self-sabotage. Why do you think you did it?

_____

_____

_____

_____

_____

_____

_____

_____

Are you ever tempted to return back to "familiar ways" that don't serve you? How did you resist that temptation? What seems to work and what doesn't?

_____

_____

_____

_____

_____

_____

_____

_____

# CHAPTER 14

*I was fascinated and thrilled,
drinking it in like a cold glass of
water after a hot day in the sun.*

## READING TIME

As you read
Chapter 14 in
*A Whole Life,*
reflect on,
and respond
to the text by
answering
the following
questions.

# REFLECT AND TAKE ACTION:

In this chapter, what kind of changes did you observe were beginning to take place in the heart and mind of the author?

_____

_____

_____

_____

_____

_____

_____

_____

_____

Do you think there is a link between the author's willingness to open the door for the two women and the tumult of his past? Elaborate.

_____

_____

_____

_____

_____

_____

_____

_____

_____

Reflect on the author's encounter with God in this chapter. In what ways has God shown you that your sin is not too big for His forgiveness?

_____

_____

_____

_____

_____

_____

_____

_____

_____

Where in the author's visit to the church do you see shame attempting to take hold of him? What do you think Jesus would tell him about his lack of "qualification"?

_____

_____

_____

_____

_____

_____

_____

_____

What kind of experiences, if any, have you had with fasting? If you have never fasted, what kind of resistance comes up for you?

_____

_____

_____

_____

_____

_____

_____

_____

_____

Whose forgiveness are you needing? Have you reached out and asked them for it? Why or why not?

_____

_____

_____

_____

_____

_____

_____

_____

_____

# CHAPTER 15

Too many times we miss important
clues people give us because we
are not really paying attention
to what they are saying—it's all
about what we want to say.

## READING TIME

As you read Chapter 15 in *A Whole Life*, reflect on, and respond to the text by answering the following questions.

# REFLECT AND TAKE ACTION:

Reflect on a time when you were thrust into a challenging situation similar to the author's door-to-door visits. How did you respond, and what did you learn? What would you change?

_____

_____

_____

_____

_____

_____

_____

_____

Consider the concept of discipline as described in this chapter. How does discipline play a role in your daily life, and in what areas could you benefit from more discipline?

_____

_____

_____

_____

_____

_____

_____

_____

_____

The author talks about the importance of making connections with others before sharing the gospel with them. Reflect on your approach to building connections with the lost. How do you establish rapport with them?

_____

_____

_____

_____

_____

_____

_____

_____

Think about a time when you faced rejection or hostility similar to the author's experiences during his visits. How has this impacted you? In what ways has it produced greater resilience?

_____

_____

_____

_____

_____

_____

_____

Reflect on the idea of serving others without seeking recognition, as the author strived to do. Compare your experiences of serving for the goal of recognition to times you have served without strings attached.

_____

_____

_____

_____

_____

_____

_____

The chapter ends with the author recognizing the need for personal growth and forgiveness. How have you changed along your journey, and who are the people who have helped you along the way? What would it have been like without them?

_____

_____

_____

_____

_____

_____

_____

_____

# CHAPTER 16

*It felt like whatever was surrounding me lifted as soon as I walked back into the house.*

## READING TIME

As you read
Chapter 16 in
*A Whole Life*,
reflect on,
and respond
to the text by
answering
the following
questions.

# REFLECT AND TAKE ACTION:

Recall a time when you learned a valuable life lesson from a seemingly simple interaction with someone, similar to when the stranger offered the author a cookie. How have you put that lesson to work in your life today?

_____

_____

_____

_____

_____

_____

_____

_____

What was your gut reaction to the author's mother's decision to sell his bed? Why do you think you reacted this way, and what other conclusions can you draw that you may have not considered?

_____

_____

_____

_____

_____

_____

_____

_____

Drawing from the collection of stories about the author's mother up to this point, how might you reframe or revise your assumptions about seemingly callous or irresponsible people? Think of someone you know or used to know who fits this description and revise your story about them.

_____

_____

_____

_____

_____

_____

_____

_____

What kind of skill sets have you acquired that were modeled to you growing up? What was your relationship with that person like?

_____

_____

_____

_____

_____

_____

_____

The author shares a transformative encounter with God that changed the direction of his life. Reflect on a pivotal moment in your life that significantly altered your path. How has that moment shaped your beliefs and actions?

_____

_____

_____

_____

_____

_____

_____

At the conclusion of this chapter, the author talks about the challenges he faced reintegrating into his old life after his mission. What kind of transitional moments have taught you the most about yourself and God?

_____

_____

_____

_____

_____

_____

_____

_____

# CHAPTER 17

*When I headed out for work in the dark,
I thought, God, if Kim is still here when
I get back later, I'll know without a
shadow of a doubt that she's the one.*

*She was, and I did.*

As you read
Chapter 17 in
*A Whole Life*,
reflect on,
and respond
to the text by
answering
the following
questions.

# REFLECT AND TAKE ACTION:

Who in your life did you have an instant deep connection with? How has that person brought you closer to God? What binds you together?

_____

_____

_____

_____

_____

_____

_____

_____

_____

Both Kim and the author were made privy to their future together prior to starting a relationship. What does that reveal to you about God?

_____

_____

_____

_____

_____

_____

_____

_____

_____

_____

Select a person in your life whom you deeply care for. How did God prepare you for a relationship with that specific person? What do you think that relationship is preparing you for now?

_____

_____

_____

_____

_____

_____

_____

The author had to confront and overcome flawed views on Christian partnership and marriage. How have you handled conflicting perspectives between you and someone important in the past? Would you have done anything differently, and if so, what?

_____

_____

_____

_____

_____

_____

_____

_____

Despite initial challenges, the author and Kim's relationship grew through them, and they came out better and stronger. What do you think enabled them to use disagreements to their advantage?

_____

_____

_____

_____

_____

_____

_____

_____

On the surface, it would seem the author's life would disqualify him from the hope of a better future. How does the author's story in this chapter encourage you?

_____

_____

_____

_____

_____

_____

_____

_____

# CHAPTER 18

*Kim wasn't having any of it. She reminded me we had both prayed about this opportunity and felt like it was something we should pursue.*

## READING TIME

As you read
Chapter 18 in
*A Whole Life*,
reflect on,
and respond
to the text by
answering
the following
questions.

# REFLECT AND TAKE ACTION:

In what ways can you relate to
the author's brief moment of
disappointment over his family's
absence at his wedding? What does his
adjusted response tell you about the
power of reframing disappointment?

_____

_____

_____

_____

_____

_____

_____

_____

What unique testimony has come out of
your history? How does your life reflect
the transformative power and goodness
of God?

_____

_____

_____

_____

_____

_____

_____

_____

_____

God opened an unexpected door for the author to begin a career in the insurance industry. How has God provided for you in ways that surprised you?

_____

_____

_____

_____

_____

_____

_____

_____

_____

What do you see more clearly now about the story God is writing for you that you didn't see before?

_____

_____

_____

_____

_____

_____

_____

_____

_____

The author failed his licensing exams several times before passing. Why do you think he continued to persevere?

_____

_____

_____

_____

_____

_____

_____

_____

_____

Do you feel like you are hitting a wall in any particular area of your life? When has resistance and opposition tempted you to throw in the towel? Did you, and what was the outcome?

_____

_____

_____

_____

_____

_____

_____

_____

_____

# CHAPTER 19

*I reminded myself that every no I got took me one call closer to my next yes.*

READING
TIME

As you read
Chapter 19 in
*A Whole Life*,
reflect on,
and respond
to the text by
answering
the following
questions.

# REFLECT AND TAKE ACTION:

The author identifies "doggedness" as the attribute that set him apart in his efforts to flourish in his new career. What sets you apart from the pack? Where do you make up for what you lack?

_____

_____

_____

_____

_____

_____

_____

_____

What role does thinking outside the box play in setting yourself apart in every area of life (work, ministry, marriage, parenthood, etc.)? How do you use creativity for greater impact and fulfillment in each domain?

_____

_____

_____

_____

_____

_____

_____

_____

To what extent do you prioritize relationship-building over business-as-usual practices in your daily responsibilities? What are some practical ways you could begin to shift your priorities in favor of relationships?

_____

_____

_____

_____

_____

_____

_____

_____

Describe how the author's persistence positively impacted his clients. Does this change your perception of persistence in any way, even when it is uncomfortable?

_____

_____

_____

_____

_____

_____

_____

_____

Identify every part of the author's story leading up to this point that prepared him for a successful future in selling insurance. How do the more adversarial parts of your story make you the right person for what God has or is calling you to?

_____

_____

_____

_____

_____

_____

_____

What inspires you most about the author's journey from having little to outperforming all past and present insurance agents at that time? Where do you see yourself in this story?

_____

_____

_____

_____

_____

_____

_____

_____

# CHAPTER 20

*People are putting their lives and the lives of their families in my hands, in a sense, and they need to be confident they can trust me.*

## READING TIME

As you read Chapter 20 in *A Whole Life*, reflect on, and respond to the text by answering the following questions.

# REFLECT AND TAKE ACTION:

Who in your life has supported and rallied around you through what felt like an impossible feat?

_____

_____

_____

_____

_____

_____

_____

_____

_____

_____

What did they offer that you could not offer on your own?

_____

_____

_____

_____

_____

_____

_____

_____

_____

_____

What have you learned about the kind of support you need most to persist when things get hard? Elaborate.

_____

_____

_____

_____

_____

_____

_____

_____

_____

_____

What did you learn about your biggest support systems that you didn't know before, and how has it shaped your relationship with them?

_____

_____

_____

_____

_____

_____

_____

_____

_____

_____

_____

How did the author's hard work pay off far beyond financial security for him and his family? What kind of payoffs do you see in your own work?

_____

_____

_____

_____

_____

_____

_____

_____

_____

_____

What did this chapter teach you about the value of transparency in relationships and business? In what ways has transparency, either your own or someone else's, impacted you?

_____

_____

_____

_____

_____

_____

_____

_____

_____

_____

The author suggests that if you aren't interested in what you are selling, then others won't be, either. What do others see when you are in action? Do they see someone who believes in what they are "selling"?

_____

_____

_____

_____

_____

_____

_____

_____

What do you do to go above and beyond in the most important areas of your life? What would going the extra mile look like for you?

_____

_____

_____

_____

_____

_____

_____

_____

# NOTES

_____
_____
_____
_____
_____
_____
_____
_____
_____
_____
_____
_____
_____
_____
_____
_____
_____
_____
_____
_____
_____
_____
_____
_____

# CHAPTER 21

*One thing I am certain of is that whatever hardships we face, they don't have to define us.*

As you read
Chapter 21 in
*A Whole Life*,
reflect on,
and respond
to the text by
answering
the following
questions.

# REFLECT AND TAKE ACTION:

The author's complicated history ends with a platform to serve and protect thousands of families around the country. In what ways is hope for others embedded in your story?

_____

_____

_____

_____

_____

_____

_____

How can keeping others in mind who need our messy stories help you walk through every trial with greater grace, peace, and joy?

_____

_____

_____

_____

_____

_____

_____

_____

_____

Whose story has inspired you to action or impacted your life in some way?

_____

_____

_____

_____

_____

_____

_____

_____

_____

The author references the necessity of uncomfortable conversations through his encounter with a widow. On a scale from 1 (not at all) to 5 (extremely), how well do you navigate uncomfortable conversations?

_____

_____

_____

_____

_____

_____

_____

_____

When has an uncomfortable conversation preserved or enriched a relationship of yours or bore fruit in some other way?

_____

_____

_____

_____

_____

_____

_____

_____

Coming upon the conclusion, in what way does the book title A Whole Life embody the author's message as a whole?

_____

_____

_____

_____

_____

_____

_____

_____

_____

www.ingramcontent.com/pod-product-compliance
Lightning Source LLC
Chambersburg PA
CBHW062118080426
42734CB00012B/2903